English: **Good morning**
GOOD MOR - NING

AF726966

Spanish: **Buenos días**
BWEN - OS ***DEE*** *- AHS*

Italian: **Buongiorno**
BWON - JORR - NO

French: **Bonjour**
BON - SHJUR

German: **Guten morgen**
GOO - TEN MOR - GEN

English: **Hello**
HEH - LOW

Spanish: **Hola**
O - LAH

Italian: **Ciao**
CHOW

French: **Bonjour**
BON - SHJUR

German: **Guten Tag**
GOO - TEN TAHK

English: **Goodbye**
GOOD - BI

Spanish: **Adiós**
AH - DEEOS

Italian: **Arrivederci**
AH - REEV - AH - DERR - CHEE

French: **Au revoir**
O REV - WAH

German: **Auf Wiedersehen**
OWF VEE - DER - SAY - EN

Pronunciation Guides

Special pronunciation guides will be underlined and color coded throughout the book.

RR = *Sounds like a purring cat,* **"RRR."**

SHJ = a combination of shhh and j. *Sounds like the* **"j"** *in de***j***a-vu.*

EH = *Sounds like the* **"e"** *in* **e***gg.*

AH = *with doctor, saying* **"ahhh."**

UH = *Sounds like the* **"u"** *in* **"under."**

CH = *Sounds like* **"ch"** *in* **"choo choo."**

KH = Whisper sound made by almost closing back of throat.

If the syllable is ***bold***, emphasis is placed on that syllable.

FRENCH and GERMAN "R's" are made by using the back of the throat.

Super Smart Language Series: AT SCHOOL
ISBN: 978-1-941775-13-4
April Chloe Terrazas, BS University of Texas at Austin.

Visit us on the web! www.Crazy-Brainz.com

Cover design, illustrations and text by: April Chloe Terrazas

<u>English:</u> **Please**
PLEEZ

<u>Spanish:</u> **Por favor**
PORR FAH - VORR

<u>Italian:</u> **Per favore**
PEHRR FAH - VORR - EH

<u>French:</u> **Se il vous plaît**
SEH EEL VOO PLAY

<u>German:</u> **Bitte**
BIT - TUH

<u>English:</u> **Thank you**
THANK U

<u>Spanish:</u> **Gracias**
GRRAH - SEE - AHS

<u>Italian:</u> **Grazie**
GRRAH - TZEE

<u>French:</u> **Merci**
MEHR - SEE

<u>German:</u> **Danke**
DAHN - KUH

English: **Backpack**

BAK - PAK

Spanish: **Mochila**

MO - CHEE - LAH

Italian: **Zaino**

ZAY - NO

French: **Sac à dos**

*SAHK - **AH** - DOS*

German: **Rucksack**

RUUK - SAHK

English: **Paper**

PAY - PR

Spanish: **Papel**

PAH - PEL

Italian: **Carta**

KARR *- TAH*

French: **Papier**

PAH *- PYAY*

German: **Papier**

PAH - ***PE*** *- UH*

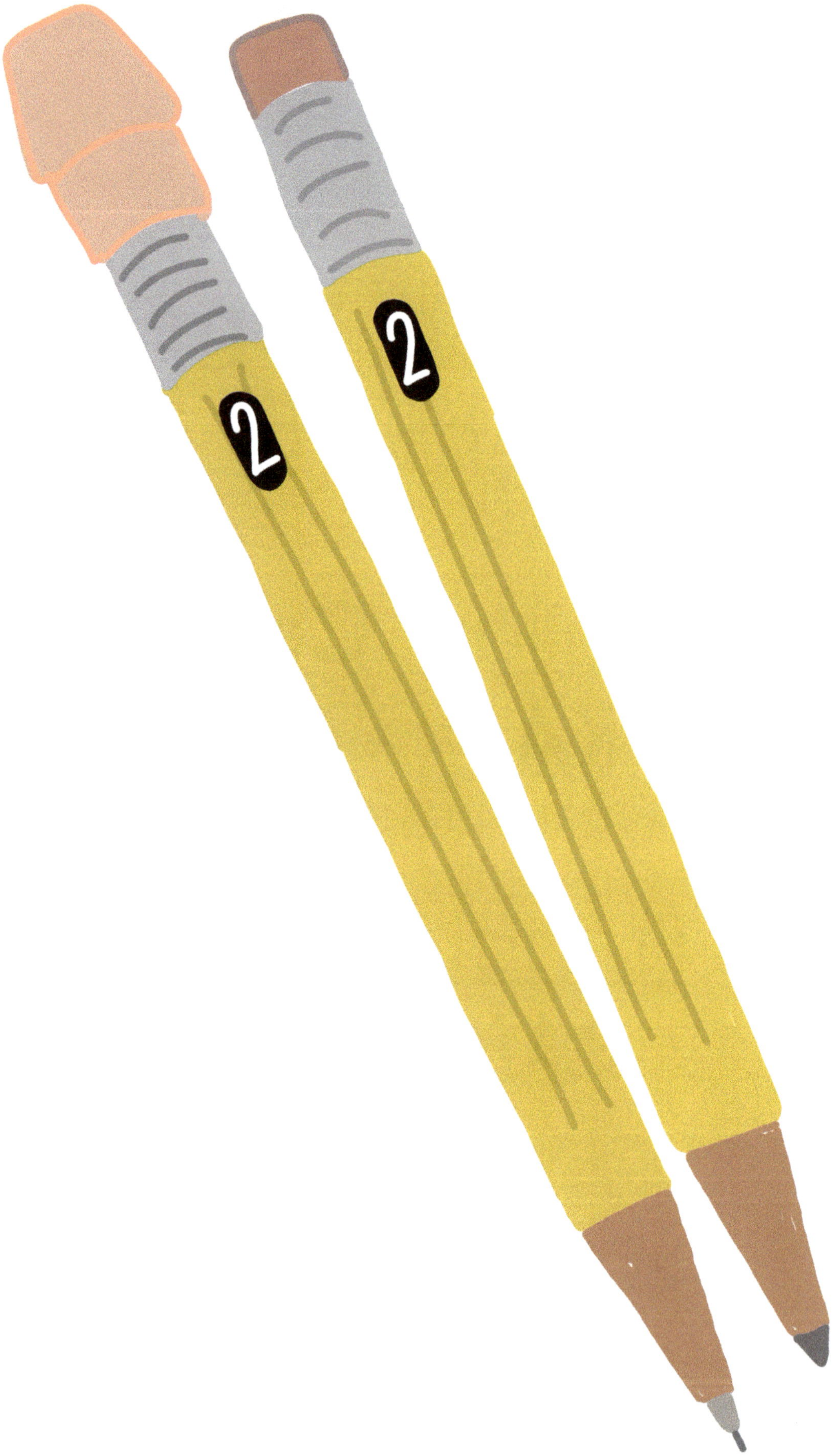
2
2

English: **Pencil**

PEN - SIL

Spanish: **Lápiz**

***L**AH - PEES*

Italian: **Matite**

MAH - TEE - TEH

French: **Crayon**

KRAY - OHN

German: **Bleistift**

BLI - SHTFT

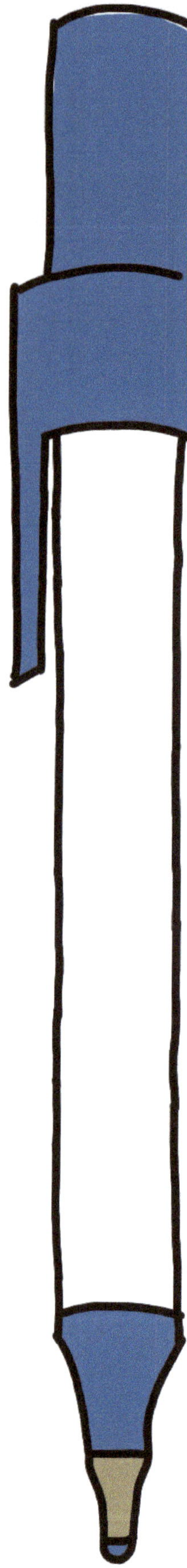

English: **Pen**

PEN

Spanish: **Pluma**

PLU - MAH

Italian: **Penna**

PEN - NAH

French: **Stylo**

STEE - LO

German: **Stift**

SHTFT

English: **Colored pencils**

KUH - LURD PEN - SILS

Spanish: **Lápices de colores**

LAH - PEES - ES DEH
KO - LORR - ES

Italian: **Matite colorate**

MAH - TEE - TEH
KO - LORR - AH - TEH

French: **Crayons de couleur**

KRAY - OHN DUH
KOO - LUR

German: **Farbstifte**

FARB - SHTFT - TEH

1
2
3
4
5
6

English: **Ruler**

ROO - LER

Spanish: **Regla**

RREG - LAH

Italian: **Righello**

*RRE - **GEL** - LO*

French: **Règle**

REHG *- LUH*

German: **Lineal**

LEE - NE - AL

12
1
2
3
4
5
6
7
8
9
10
11

English: **Clock**

KLOK

Spanish: **Reloj**

RREH - LO

Italian: **Orologio**

*ORR - O - **LO** - JO*

French: **Horloge**

OR - LOSHJ

German: **Uhr**

OOUH

English: **Book**

BOOK

Spanish: **Libro**

LEE - BRRO

Italian: **Libro**

***LEE** - BRRO*

French: **Livre**

LEE - VRUH

German: **Buch**

BUUKH

7
8
9
CE
4
5
6
×
M+
1
2
3
–
M-
0
•
÷
+
=

English: **Calculator**

KAL - KU - LA - TR

Spanish: **Calculadora**

KAL - Q - LAH - DORR - AH

Italian: **Calcolatrice**

KAL - KO - LAH - TRREE - CHEH

French: **Calculatrice**

KAL - Q - LAH - TREES

German: **Rechner**

REKH - NAH

English: **Glue**

GLU

Spanish: **Pegamento**

PEG - AH - MEN - TO

Italian: **Colla**

KO - LAH

French: **Colle**

KOLUH

German: **Klebstoff**

KLEEB - SHTOFF

English: **Notebook**
NOTE - BOOK

Spanish: **Cuaderno**
CUAH - DERR - NO

Italian: **Taccuino**
TAH - QUEE - NO

French: **Cahier**
KAH EEYAY

German: **Heft**
HEFT

English: **Scissors**

SIZ - ERZ

Spanish: **Tijeras**

TEE - HERR - AHS

Italian: **Forbici**

FORR *- BEE - CHEE*

French: **Ciseaux**

SEE - ZO

German: **Schere**

SHEER - UH

English: **Bathroom**

BATH - ROOM

Spanish: **Cuarto de baño**

QUARRTO DEH BAHN - YO

Italian: **Bagno**

BAHN - YO

French: **Salle de bain**

SAL - DUH - BAHN

German: **Toilette**

TWAH - LET

English: **Chair**

CHAIR

Spanish: **Silla**

SEE - YAH

Italian: **Sedia**

***SED** - EE - YAH*

French: **Chaise**

SHEHZ

German: **Stuhl**

SHTOO - WEL

Chalkboard

English: **Chalkboard**

CHALK - BORD

Spanish: **Pizarra**

PEEZ - ARR - AH

Italian: **Lavagna**

LAH - VAHN - YAH

French: **Tableau**

TAHB - LO

German: **Tafel**

TAH - FEL

English: **Trash**

TRASH

Spanish: **Basura**

BAH - SURR - AH

Italian: **Cestino**

CHES - TEE - NO

French: **Poubelle**

POO - BEL

German: **Müll**

MUHL

English: **Music, Art**

MU - ZIK, ART

Spanish: **Música, Arte**

MOO *- SEE - KAH, ARR - TEH*

Italian: **Musica, Arte**

MOO - ZEE - KAH, ARR - TEH

French: **Musique, Classe d'art**

MOO - ZEE - KUH,

KLASS DAHR

German: **Musik, Kunst**

MOO - ZEEK, KOONST

www.ingramcontent.com/pod-product-compliance
Ingram Content Group UK Ltd.
Pitfield, Milton Keynes, MK11 3LW, UK
UKHW062001290726
14090UKWH00021B/1332

9 781941 775134